Ben the Bear
and the
Honey-Suckle Tree

Merry Christmas
Jack

Jay Conley

Illustrations by Steve Rabatich of Studio Saskatoon
Color Digitization by Jonathan Petryk
Printed by Houghton Boston, Saskatoon Canada

Canadian Cataloguing in Publication Data

Conley, Samuel James, 1959-
    Ben the Bear and the Honey-Suckle Tree
ISBN: 0-9687524-0-3

I. Rabatich, Steve II. Title. III. Series: Conley, Samuel James, 1959- .
    Honey-Suckle Tree Collection.

PS8555.05374B45 2000   jc813'.6   C00-901228-1
PZ7.C761842Ben 2000

Published by   UNITE OUR DREAMS
                        PUBLICATIONS

Ben the Bear
and the
Honey-Suckle Tree

Dedicated to

my mother and father, Della and Jim Conley,

and to two dear friends, Carol and Brian Morrison.

Not so long ago, and not so far away, a baby bear was born to Mama and Papa Bear.

They named him Benjamin, but everyone called him Ben for short.

As Ben was growing up, one of the great things he loved to do was to be thrown up onto Papa's big, broad back and romp through the forest trying to catch butterflies.

Now the two of them never, ever caught any butterflies, but that didn't matter. Just being thrown up on Papa's back and being with him is what really counted.

One day when they were romping through the forest,
Ben heard some crying. He looked down and saw,
on one side of a huge rock, three little bunnies.
Ben just knew they were lost.

Ben was up high enough on Papa's back to see, on the other side of the
rock, Mama Rabbit playing with her other little ones.

Ben got off Papa's back,

scooped up the three bunnies,

and took them around to the other side.

Rhonda Rabbit was filled with joy.

She had so many children, she hadn't noticed

these three were missing just yet.

One day Ben felt especially happy. It was the first time in his life Papa said he could stay up past his bedtime. As the moon rose the two of them made their way to William Wolf's den.

Ben was surprised to see all the other animals of the forest there that night.

You see, Ben had never seen the animals of the evening before.

William Wolf spoke about how all the animals of the forest are related. In fact, William said the whole forest is woven together.

He spoke of the great hope he had for all the animals, and something about courage, peace, and happiness coming from within. Ben wasn't too sure about this courage and peace kind of stuff just yet, but boy was it great to be part of the group!

The greatest thing of all Ben loved to do was visit the Honey-Suckle Tree. Now the Honey-Suckle Tree is the only tree like it in the whole forest. There is no other like this one.

The Honey-Suckle Tree is in the very center of the forest and is very old, huge, and gnarly. It takes twenty adult bears with their paws tip to tip to go around it.

Out of the Honey-Suckle Tree flowed the golden honey-suckle. It sparkled like diamonds. It flowed out of the tree, down the trunk, and into the creeks. The creeks would deliver it to the river.

Every tree in the forest has its roots tied into the river, so the honey-suckle would flow up their roots and into the berries. The birds would eat the berries and their sweet songs would fill the forest. The animals would eat the berries and their furs would shine.

Ben loved going straight to the source, the Honey-Suckle Tree, with Papa Bear. They would take both their paws, fill their faces with honey-suckle, and their furs sparkled.

As Ben got a little older, he didn't listen to Papa quite so much. He started to hang out and play with Billy Badger. Now Billy never visited the center of the forest; he always played at the outer edges.

One day when they were out playing, Billy said, "throwing rocks is fun." The two of them scooped up some rocks and threw them into Rebecca and Roy Robin's nest, breaking the eggs. Ben didn't think that was too much fun, but because Billy had said it was…he went along with it.

Some time later, Billy just up and said, "It's the one who has the most acorns in the end that wins." The two of them made a plan and they went off to Sam Squirrel's place.

Out in front of Sam's place, Ben pretended to be sick. When Sam came out to offer his help, Billy slipped inside and stole all of Sam's acorns. Ben and Billy didn't know what to do with acorns at the time, but that didn't matter. Remember, it was what Billy had said: "It's the one with the most acorns in the end that wins."

Another time, Ben and Billy were play-wrestling.
Sally Skunk, just wanting to make some new friends,
came up and asked, "Hey! Can I play with you guys?"
Ben was about to say, "Yeah, come and play with us,"
but before he did, he looked over his shoulder
to see what Billy would say.

Billy pointed a paw at her and said, "You're stinky!" As Sally ran away crying, Billy started to laugh. Ben didn't think this was quite right, but because Billy was laughing, well, Ben laughed too.

There actually came a day that Ben became sick. Not pretend sick. This time he was really sick! It was the first time in a long time that Ben looked at himself. When he did, he noticed that he no longer sparkled like diamonds. That was the day he remembered the Honey-Suckle Tree. You see, Ben had forgotten all about it. So, that very day Ben decided to visit the tree once again.

On his way there, Ben noticed that the birds were not singing like they used to. In fact, the whole forest had become a dull gray.

When Ben got to the river, he saw that the river had all but dried up. He kept on going.

When he got to the center of the forest, Ben saw that although the whole forest had become a dull gray, the Honey-Suckle Tree hadn't changed. The tree itself remained the same.

The difference was that
the honey-suckle, which
once flowed, was now going
drip...drip...drip...

Ben sat down at the base of the tree and thought. He thought long and hard, back to the time when the honey-suckle flowed. Back to the time when he was romping through the forest on Papa's back. Back to the time when he was part of the group at William Wolf's den. Back to the time when he helped out Rhonda Rabbit.

Ben came to understand that the honey-suckle flows when the relationship with the Tree of Life is right. When there is faith, hope and love.

All of a sudden, the honey-suckle that was once dripping started to swooosh…swooosh…swooosh…

This is the first of many stories of Ben, his friends and the Honey-Suckle Tree.

Now you should know, boys and girls, that not all Billy's are like that, and not all badgers are like that. It just happens in this story, Billy is a badger.

The story of "Ben the Bear and the Honey-Suckle Tree" is the first part in a series of the Honey-Suckle Tree Collection. The following questions are examples of questions the author asks when leading a classroom in discussion. You may want to lead a discussion with your own children.

1   What kind of other animals were at William Wolf's den? (Remember that it was nighttime and Ben had never seen these animals before).

2   What do you think Ben did when he first met these new animals of the forest?

3   What is the great hope William Wolf spoke of?

4   Why did Ben go along with Billy? He knew their actions were wrong.

5   Was it a cool thing to try to be like Billy?

6   What happened to Ben as a result of his choices and actions?

7   What happened to the rest of the forest?

8   Is the honey-suckle going to come back as it was in the beginning of the story?

9   What will it take to bring the honey-suckle back?

10 How can Ben and the other animals help Billy?

11 Can you think of some ways you could help someone who is like Billy Badger?

12 When does the honey-suckle flow?

We welcome you to share your comments with Ben @ e-mail: ben@benthebear.com
Or mail: *Honey-Suckle Tree Collection*
               P.O. Box 22140 RPO Wildwood
               Saskatoon SK Canada S7H 5P1

Please include your name, age, and city you live in. As well, please indicate whether we may use your comments in future stories and projects.
You may wish to visit our web-site at: www.benthebear.com